EARLY BRITISH HISTORY

The Viking and Anglo-Saxon Struggle for England

Claire Throp

Raintree is an imprint of Capstone Global Library Limited, a company incorporated in England and Wales having its registered office at 7 Pilgrim Street, London, EC4V 6LB – Registered company number: 6695582

www.raintree.co.uk
myorders@raintree.co.uk

Edited by Helen Cox-Cannons and Holly Beaumont
Designed by Richard Parker
Original illustrations © Capstone Global Library Limited 2015
Illustrated by Martin Sanders (Beehive Illustration)
Picture research by Svetlana Zhurkin and Pam Mitsakos
Production by Helen McCreath
Originated by Capstone Global Library Limited
Printed and bound in China by CTPS

ISBN 978 1 406 29109 4 (hardback)
18 17 16 15 14
10 9 8 7 6 5 4 3 2 1

ISBN 978 1 406 29114 8 (paperback)
19 18 17 16 15
10 9 8 7 6 5 4 3 2 1

British Library Cataloguing in Publication Data
A full catalogue record for this book is available from the British Library.

Acknowledgements
We would like to thank the following for permission to reproduce photographs: Alamy: 19th era, 27, ArtPix, 21, Chris Gibson, 17, Colin Underhill, 26, Jorge Royan, 29, Mary Evans Picture Library, 15, Simon Belcher, 11; Bridgeman Images: Ashmolean Museum, University of Oxford, UK, 28; Corbis: Bettmann, 5, Hulton-Deutsch Collection, 19, Stapleton Collection, 10; Getty Images: Popperfoto, 18, Print Collector, 25, UIG/Hoberman Collection, 24; iStockphotos: duncan1890, 12; Newscom: akg-images/British Library, 14, 23; Shutterstock: Danny Smythe, cover inset (ship), David Lochhead, 20, Heartland Arts, cover, Hyena Reality, background (throughout), Karramba Production, cover (top left), back cover, Stanislav Petrov, background (throughout), Steve Silver Smith, 4, Vadim Sadovski, 6—7 (back).

We would like to thank Dr Mark Zumbuhl of the University of Oxford for his invaluable help in the preparation of this book.

Every effort has been made to contact copyright holders of material reproduced in this book. Any omissions will be rectified in subsequent printings if notice is given to the publisher.

Contents

Some words in this book appear in bold, **like this.** You can find out what they mean by looking in the glossary.

Early Viking raids

In the late 700s, Britain was made up of different **kingdoms**. The Picts lived in Pictland, which covered most of the north and east of what is now Scotland. The Gaels lived in Dál Riata, in the west of what is now Scotland. They originally came from Ireland, and were also called the Scoti or Scots.

Wales was divided into Gwynedd, Powys, Gwent and Glamorgan, and Deheubarth. In England, the three biggest kingdoms were Mercia, Wessex and Northumbria. There were also four smaller kingdoms: Sussex, East Anglia, Essex and Kent. You can see all of these on the map on page 9. At the time of the first Viking attacks, Mercia was the most powerful of the English kingdoms.

Viking raids

The first Viking attack came in 787 when three Viking **longships** attacked southern England. Later, people were shocked when the Vikings attacked the **monastery** of Lindisfarne (below) in 793. These early **raids** were mainly for **plunder** – not to find somewhere to live.

THE VIKINGS

The Vikings came from three main countries: Denmark, Norway and Sweden (see map on page 9). They travelled across the sea in long, narrow ships called longships. Vikings from Denmark and Sweden mainly attacked and settled in England. Vikings from Norway invaded Scotland. Few Vikings settled in Wales.

ALCUIN

A monk called Alcuin wrote to the king of Northumbria about the attack on Lindisfarne. He wrote of the horror people felt at the destruction of a **Christian** monastery. The Vikings were not Christian, so they would only have been interested in the valuable items that they could steal.

TIMELINE

The Viking **invasion** and settlement of Britain happened over a number of years. This timeline will help you see what happened when.

> For an explanation of what AD and BC mean, please see the glossary on page 30.

787
The first Viking **raids** on England take place

793
Vikings attack the **monastery** of Lindisfarne

866
Vikings **conquer** Northumbria, including the city of York

870
Vikings attack Wessex, the last Anglo-Saxon **kingdom** not under Viking control

871
Battle of Ashdown. King Ethelred and his brother Alfred defeat the Vikings.

871
Alfred becomes king

876
Vikings begin to settle in England

Alfred defeats the Vikings at the Battle of Edington.

886
A **treaty** between the Vikings and Alfred divides the country into Alfred's lands and land controlled by the Vikings. This later becomes known as the Danelaw.

925
Athelstan becomes king

937
Battle of Brunanburh. Athelstan defeats the British, Scots and Vikings and becomes king of all England.

980
A new period of Viking attacks on England

991
Ethelred starts to pay a tribute of money (the Danegeld) to the Vikings to stop them attacking

1013
Sweyn becomes England's first Viking king

1042
Edward the Confessor becomes king of England

1066
Edward the Confessor dies

Invasion

In the late 790s and early 800s, Vikings attacked the Scottish islands of Orkney and Iona. Little is known about these attacks because the **monasteries** were burnt and the monks living there were the only people who would have written about the **raids**. Most people could not read or write at the time.

The Anglo-Saxon **kingdoms** were nearly always fighting each other rather than working together to fight the Vikings, so the Viking attacks continued. It is thought that Vikings were already beginning to settle in places such as Jarlshof on the Scottish island of Shetland in the 800s.

WHAT'S THE LANGUAGE?

Old Norse was the language spoken by the Vikings. It was similar to the Old English spoken by the Anglo-Saxons. Some of the words we use today come from Old Norse, such as anger from *angr*, knife from *knifr* and die from *deyja*.

deyja

knifr

Larger armies

From the 850s Vikings began to spend the winter in Britain, while continuing to **plunder** nearby areas. They began to bring larger armies to Britain from around 865. It was clear that they wanted to **conquer** the country, not just plunder it. In 866, they took Northumbria, including the city of York (which was then in Northumbria).

After conquering East Anglia during 869–870, the Vikings attacked Wessex, the last remaining independent Anglo-Saxon kingdom. It was in Wessex that they met their match.

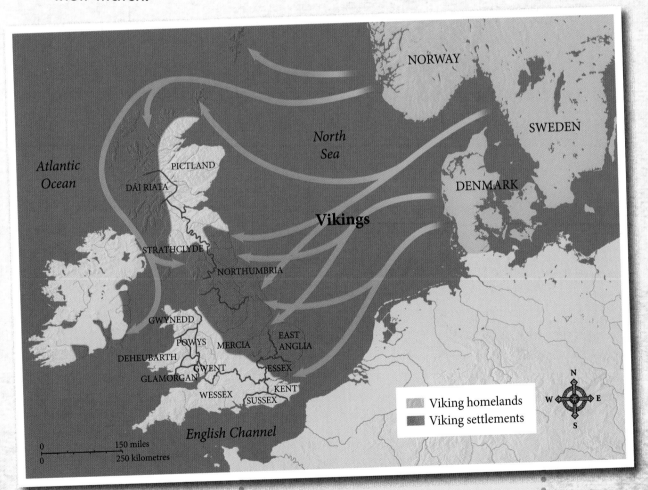

This map shows where the Vikings came from and which parts of Britain and Ireland they settled in.

Fighting back

The Vikings were based in Reading when they planned to **conquer** the **kingdom** of Wessex. In January 871, the Battle of Ashdown took place. King Ethelred and his brother Alfred defeated the Vikings and drove them back to Reading.

Mixing with the Anglo-Saxons

From the mid-870s, Vikings begin to settle and farm in the lands they had conquered in the north and east of England. They began to mix with the Anglo-Saxons. Old Norse words were taken up by the Anglo-Saxons, and towns were given Norse names such as Jorvik (now known as York).

The Battle of Ashdown began while Alfred was in charge. King Ethelred had gone to church.

WHAT'S THE LANGUAGE?

Many of the place names in Britain are from the Viking age. Places ending in –by, such as Derby, meant farms or villages. Places that end in -throp, -thorp or -thorpe meant farms.

More defeats

Just two weeks later, though, the Vikings won a battle at Basing. They were helped by the arrival in Reading of a second group of Vikings. In April, King Ethelred was badly injured and died. Alfred became king. Nine major battles took place during 871, and the Vikings won many of them. It is thought that Alfred eventually managed to keep the Vikings away only by giving them money.

Alfred was just 21 when he became king.

Forced out of Wessex

In early January 878, the Vikings, led by Guthrum, surprised Alfred while he was in Chippenham. It was a **Christian** holiday, so the Anglo-Saxons would not have been expecting an attack. Alfred escaped but was forced to hide in marshland in Somerset. The king struggled to survive for weeks with little to eat.

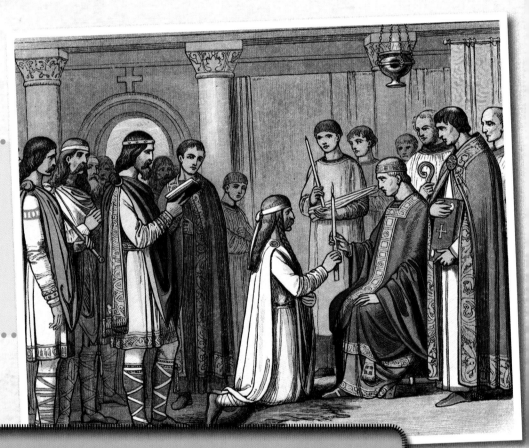

This illustration shows Guthrum being baptised into the Christian religion.

GUTHRUM

Guthrum was the Viking leader who fought against Alfred for control of Wessex. It is thought he first came to England in the **invasion** of 865. After defeat at Edington, Guthrum settled in East Anglia, and ruled from 880 until his death in 890.

This map shows how Britain was divided into Anglo-Saxon lands and the Danelaw. People living in the Danelaw followed Viking customs and spoke Old Norse.

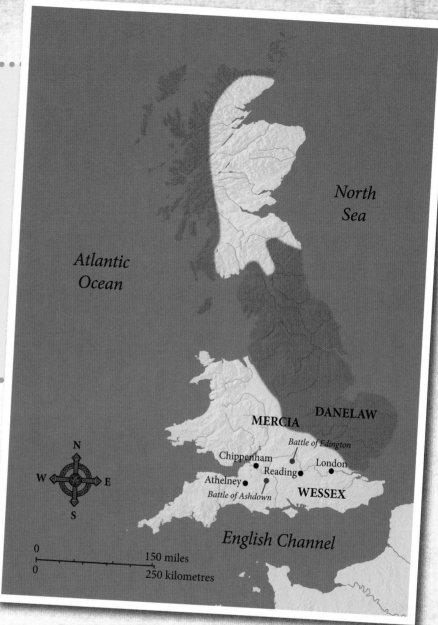

Battle of Edington

In spring 878, Alfred built a **fort** at Athelney and made **raids** against the Vikings. Eventually, he built up enough of an army to defeat the Vikings in the Battle of Edington in May 878. After the battle, the two sides discussed making peace. Alfred knew the Vikings weren't going to go away so he tried to encourage peace by holding feasts and celebrations. Guthrum agreed to become a Christian, as did many other Vikings. In 886, England was divided into Anglo-Saxon lands and the Danelaw – land ruled by the Vikings.

Alfred's reign

Alfred was now accepted as king of all English people, except those living under Viking rule. He took the chance to make changes to his **kingdom** while there were no Viking attacks.

THE ANGLO-SAXON CHRONICLE AND ASSER

The Anglo-Saxon Chronicle is a history of England, and the first to be written in English. It was begun in 890 during Alfred's **reign** and was added to until the mid-1100s. This section (right) was written in 1058–59. We also know about Alfred's reign from a Welsh monk called Asser. He wrote *Life of King Alfred* in 893.

Defences

Alfred reorganized the army and Anglo-Saxon defences so that they would be better prepared for the next Viking attack. He encouraged the building of **forts** and towns. He also built a navy of fast ships.

Alfred brought together **laws** made by other kings, including Offa. He decided which laws to keep and which not to keep after talking to his **advisers**.

Education and religion

Alfred tried to improve the education of his people by encouraging boys to go to school so that they could at least read English. The Viking **raids** on **monasteries** meant that few could read or write Latin by this time. Alfred even **translated** a number of books from Latin to English himself after learning Latin in his late 30s. He also set up new monasteries, hoping to increase the number of monks who could read and write.

Continuing the fight

Alfred arranged for his daughter Aethelflaed to marry a Mercian ruler, which helped to bring Mercia and Wessex together. After Alfred's death in 899, his son Edward became king. At this time, Vikings were in control of the north and east of England.

Gaining ground

From about 910, Aethelflaed and Edward built **forts** at the borders between their lands and the Danelaw. In 917, they made a joint push and defeated the Vikings in East Anglia. While fighting in Leicester the following year, Aethelflaed died. Edward took control of her lands in Mercia. With help from Aethelflaed, Edward had managed to gain control of the Danelaw south of the River Humber in Yorkshire.

AETHELFLAED

Aethelflaed was born in about 870. She became known as the Lady of the Mercians. She ruled Mercia from at least 911 when her husband died, and possibly a couple of years before that. She was admired and respected. Her army was happy to be led by a woman, which was unusual for the time. Aethelflaed died in 918.

This statue of Aethelflaed is outside Tamworth Castle in Staffordshire. In 913, Aethelflaed marched her army to Tamworth and ordered a fort to be built there.

More control

In 920, Edward won control of Northumbria. In 921, the Scottish kings agreed to be **loyal** to Edward. This meant they would not attack him and would support him against the Vikings. Edward now ruled over most of England. He died in 924.

The first king of England

Edward's son Aelfweard died just two weeks after his father. Athelstan, another of Edward's sons, became the next king.

Althelstan was Alfred's favourite grandson. He spent his childhood with his aunt Aethelflaed in Mercia, and grew up to be a great soldier.

Athelstan founded many **monasteries** and arranged for the Bible to be written in English.

Winning back land

After some **rebellion** against his kingship at the start of his **reign**, Athelstan eventually won the people's trust. He was an excellent soldier and took York and Northumbria from the Vikings in 927. Scottish, northern and Welsh kings agreed to be **loyal** to him. The five Welsh kings even agreed to pay Athelstan large sums of money, called tribute.

Improving his kingdom

For the next six years, Athelstan focused on improving his **kingdom.** He travelled around the country, holding meetings with the top **nobility** to discuss **laws** (see pages 22–23). He wanted to make sure he knew what was going on in his kingdom. Athelstan continued King Alfred's push to improve education and the religious life of his people. He encouraged trade to be carried out in towns. He also controlled where coins were made so that they all had the same weight of silver.

A challenge to the king

In 934, Athelstan attacked Scotland. It is not known whether this was because Constantine, a Scottish king, had broken the peace **treaty** or because Athelstan wanted to increase his power. Constantine was defeated and had to swear **loyalty** to Athelstan, but the peace did not last.

Athelstan's army trapped King Constantine II of Scotland in Dunnottar Castle in Stonehaven.

Constantine was worried that Athelstan's control over Northumbria was a threat to his **kingdom**. He joined forces with King Owain of Strathclyde and King Olaf, leader of the Vikings in Ireland, and they invaded England in 937.

Battle of Brunanburh

The Battle of Brunanburh took place in summer 937.
Athelstan defeated the army of Scots and Vikings.
The battle lasted only one day but thousands died. The
battle brought together all the local leaders in support
of Athelstan and stopped the Vikings – Olaf returned to
Ireland after the defeat. Constantine fled to Scotland.

Athelstan died in 939 and was buried in Malmesbury Abbey in Wiltshire. His remains were moved years later and this tomb, which was made later, in the 15th century, sits empty.

THE BATTLE OF BRUNANBURH

We know very little about the Battle of Brunanburh, including where it took place. Our information mainly comes from a poem in the Anglo-Saxon Chronicle called "The Battle of Brunanburh".

King of all Britain

Athelstan was a good soldier who increased English
power to a level not known before. Athelstan had coins
made with *Rex totius Britanniae* written on them. This
means "king of all Britain". He was making it clear that he
ruled over the whole of Britain.

Anglo-Saxon law

Laws are the sets of rules people follow to make sure **society** runs smoothly. The laws changed in the Viking age because society had changed. Early law was based on small groups of people living in one place, but by the 900s, laws had to cover more people over a larger area. From the 900s, crime became a crime not just against a single person but against the whole of society.

Oaths

In Anglo-Saxon times, people believed that a person's promise meant a lot – if they promised to do something, they would. An **oath**, or promise, was taken by all men from the age of 12 (apart from slaves) to say they would not commit a crime. This meant that theft, for example, was seen as an act of disloyalty. Courts were set up to decide what punishment should be given to someone who had broken the law.

HELPING THE POOR

Athelstan introduced the first laws to help the poor. If an official (such as a sheriff or earl) failed to properly provide for poor people in his area, he would have to hand out money under the watchful gaze of the local bishop.

This painting from the 11th century shows an Anglo-Saxon king with his advisers. These were men who gave the king advice on the law and helped him decide what to do with criminals.

Athelstan's views

Horrible punishments were given to people who had committed a crime, but Athelstan didn't like the large number of young people who were being killed for small crimes. He changed the law so that no child under the age of 15 could be put to death for their crime.

The beginnings of the system of **Parliament** we have today can be seen during Athelstan's **reign**. He had meetings with **advisers** from all over the country to discuss his new laws.

The last Anglo-Saxon kings

In 978, Ethelred the Unready became king at the age of seven after his supporters murdered his half-brother, Edward the Martyr. Ethelred was never a popular king.

Ethelred's nickname "the Unready" comes from the Old English word *unraed*, which means badly advised. Many people thought that he had helped in his brother's murder so some **advisers** were not **loyal** to him after Edward the Martyr's death.

Danegeld

The 980s saw more Viking **raids.** Ethelred was not a very good soldier, so he kept the Vikings away with money. He raised this money by **taxing** the English people. The tax became known as the Danegeld. By 1012, 48,000 pounds of silver had been handed over to Vikings based in London.

Sweyn of Denmark

A Viking called Sweyn of Denmark had been **conquering** parts of England since 1003. His sister had died in 1002 when Ethelred ordered all Vikings in England to be killed. England's **nobility** were fed up with Ethelred doing nothing to stop Sweyn, so in 1013 they asked Sweyn to become king. Ethelred fled to Normandy, France. After Sweyn's death in 1014, Ethelred ruled again, but he died two years later.

The Danish king

In 1016, Sweyn's son Canute became king of England. He also became king of Denmark and Norway, so he had to spend time there as well. He allowed English and Danish earls to run England while he was away.

K. CANUTE the GREAT.

Canute became king because he defeated Ethelred's son Edmund in the Battle of Ashingdon.

Edward the Confessor

Edward the Confessor was the son of Ethelred and his second wife, Emma. He had been living in Normandy while the Danish kings ruled England. In 1042, Edward was asked to return to England as king.

Edward preferred his Norman **advisers**, people he knew from his days living in France. Godwine, Earl of Wessex, was the leader of a group of men who thought this was unfair. In 1051, men in Dover rioted because they did not want to obey a Norman lord. When Edward ordered Godwine to punish them, Godwine refused. He was then **exiled** in 1051.

GODWINE, EARL OF WESSEX

Godwine was probably born in Sussex in 1001. He became one of the most powerful men in England. King Canute made him Earl of Wessex in 1018. Godwine's daughter married King Edward, but this did not prevent fighting between the two men. Godwine died in 1053.

Edward was known as "the Confessor" because he was very religious.

This illustration shows the riot in Dover in 1051. A number of men died during the riot.

Harold

Godwine raised an army while abroad and returned to England in 1052. Edward was forced to give Godwine's land back to him. After Godwine's death, his son Harold became a powerful person and he worked closely with Edward. It was Harold who defeated **rebellions** in Wales and Northumbria, not Edward.

When Edward died in January 1066, there was confusion over who would be the new king – Harold or William of Normandy. It was Harold who became king, as Harold II. This led to the Norman **invasion** of 1066 and Harold was killed at the Battle of Hastings in October. There were no more Anglo-Saxon kings after Harold.

The end of the Anglo-Saxons

Major changes took place in what is now England from the 800s to the 1000s. What happened during Alfred the Great's **reign** led to the Anglo-Saxon **kingdoms** joining to become England in Athelstan's reign. **Christianity** became the main religion of the country. The English language, books, **laws** and kingdoms were all affected by the late Anglo-Saxon period.

The Alfred Jewel is famous for having the words "Alfred ordered me to be made" written around the edge.

Scotland

The Anglo-Saxons, and particularly the Vikings, had a huge effect on the kingdom of the Picts. The kings of Dál Riata were able to take over Pictland. From about 900, this new kingdom became known as Scotland. The remaining Picts eventually took up the Gaelic language and culture so that Pictland no longer existed.

Place names show the Vikings had a strong influence in Scotland, particularly in Caithness, Orkney and Shetland. Many everyday Viking items have been found there, such as brooches and combs.

1066

The year 1066 marked a big change in England with the success of the Normans at the Battle of Hastings. Harold II was to be the last English-speaking king for 300 years.

The Cuerdale hoard is a collection of silver coins and jewellery found in Lancashire, England. It is thought to have belonged to Vikings who came over from Ireland in 902. This picture shows just some of what was found in the hoard.

Glossary

adviser someone who offers advice and suggestions about what to do

Christian someone who follows the religion that teaches about the life of Jesus Christ

conquer take control of an area or country by force

exile not allowed to live in your own country

fort building that can be defended against an enemy

invasion taking over a place or country by force

kingdom area ruled by a king

law set of rules that people follow to make sure a country runs smoothly

longship long, narrow warship used by the Vikings

loyal give support to someone

monastery place where monks live. Monks are very religious men.

nobility people at the top of society

oath promise

Parliament representatives of the people who meet to discuss laws

plunder steal goods or valuable items from a person or place

raid surprise attack

rebellion fight against a ruler or ruling group

reign period of time that a king or queen rules for

society group of people living together in an area or country that have shared laws and culture

tax money paid to the government

translate change words from one language into another

treaty written agreement

Find out more

Books

How to be an Anglo-Saxon, Scoular Anderson
  (Collins, 2011)
Life in Anglo-Saxon Britain (A Child's History of Britain),
  Anita Ganeri (Raintree, 2014)
Transport (Viking Life), Nicola Barber (Wayland, 2013)

Websites

www.bbc.co.uk/schools/primaryhistory/anglo_saxons
Discover everything you could want to know about the
Anglo-Saxons on this BBC website.

www.bbc.co.uk/schools/primaryhistory/vikings
Learn more about the Vikings on this website.

Places to visit

If you want to visit some of the places in this book, such
as Lindisfarne or Iona, find out more at the following
websites:

The National Trust in England, Wales and
  Northern Ireland
www.nationaltrust.org.uk

The National Trust in Scotland
www.nts.org.uk

English Heritage
www.english-heritage.org.uk

Index